Handfast

Scottish poems for weddings and affirmations

Introduction by
LIZ LOCHHEAD

Edited by
LIZZIE MACGREGOR

SCOTTISH POETRY LIBRARY
By leaves we live

Polygon

First published in 2004 by
The Scottish Poetry Library
5 Crichton's Close
Edinburgh EH8 8DT
in association with
POLYGON

ISBN 1 904598 24 2

The publishers acknowledge support from
the Scottish Arts Council
towards the publication of this title.

Designed and typeset in
10/14pt Foundry Sans by James Hutcheson
Printed and bound by
The Cromwell Press, Trowbridge Wiltshire

Scottish
Arts Council
LOTTERY FUNDED

My heart is yours now; keep it fast:
Without your favour my joy is past.
I will not change while my life last,
I promise you.

Extract from a poem in an anonymous
15th century manuscript, set into modern English
by MARGOT ROBERT ADAMSON

CONTENTS

'Let us be lovers and marry our fortunes together' sang Simon and Garfunkel in 1960-something. (Probably '67, almost every other thing that sings itself that clearly and over-and-over in me is from '67, that very good year, when I was 19.) 'Let us be lovers and marry our fortunes together.'

And for the longest time that was good enough for me.

But of course it's only pillow-talk of a song, a whispered declaration, a private utterance, and Marriage is Public, saying it out loud in front of our friends and families. Sooner or later many of us – even those most sceptical of man-made institutions, those who've scrupulously refused to promise the un-promisable, those who've said, 'No daft wee bit of paper could make us more committed to each other' – surprise ourselves by throwing a Wedding, or just taking the afternoon off work, grabbing a couple of strangers for witnesses outside the Registry Office and Making it Legal. Others plan and save for years for the theatrically perfect dress, and venue, and resplendent feast, strewn flower petals under our feet. Whoever we are, however we go about marking off this day from all others as special, we are making a flamboyantly romantic gesture in celebrating our own ordinary, amazing, precarious, miracle of one-on-one love with a wedding. 'Hit's clear to ilka guest/ Whit force steirs groom and bride in/ A love that's no for hidin' – as Tom

Hubbard's translation from Catullus's ancient epithalamium has it.

At our own all of a sudden, spur of the moment, let's-just-take-the-afternoon-off-and-do-this-with-half-a-dozen-guests-maximum wedding – and it wasn't yesterday, for my tiny baby nephew who, in his pastel velveteen babygro, was my beloved 'something blue' is now a towering seventeen year old – what I remember is the registrar explaining carefully how it was the saying out loud in front of witnesses that you took each other as man and wife that made you so. It wasn't the signing of the paper, it was the speaking out of the words. I remember how, literally, *awesome* I found it that I must manage to say 'I take this man, Thomas William Logan as my lawful husband'. Enough for it to strike me, quite uncharacteristically, dumb, and also with terror that if I didn't (and it wasn't looking good, I was getting more choked dumbstruck by the moment) that I would not be able to be married to this man I so very much wanted to marry. Well, I must have managed to get it said, somehow, and, no regrets, Tom, husband of my heart, who spoke out loud and clear for me, I'd say it over and over again for every day of the last seventeen years and for every day of our finite future together.

Clearly, despite the possibly excessive plainness of our nuptials, something which is normally to me as natural as breathing, that is to speak aloud a poem, would have been beyond me. But I know many of you have picked up this book in search of one, of a piece of public utterance to put into your particular and personal ceremony to make it uniquely yours. The lovely title, *Handfast*, refers to the old

Scots custom of betrothal by joining hands together in promise to live together for a year before marriage. (How utterly recognisable and modern an arrangement this sounds! How sensible!) Please find Diana Hendry and Hamish Whyte's witty and joyous 'Bidie-in' which, with its merry application for the job and glad appointment to it, glories gorgeously in the joys of not-married (yet?) love.

'There are all manner of betrothals and all are blessed so long as the heart be true.' Knowing this, the makers of this book have put together this selection of poems so you may find one to be said out loud at your own form of marrying or handfasting, whether your union is heterosexual or gay, whether legally binding or not, whether it's first, second or even third time around. Use, for instance, with all my good wishes, and theirs, the epithalamium I wrote for my friends Joe and Annie Thomson and spoke at their huge and splendid ceremony. A poem that, while utterly specific to the circumstances of their own surprising, life-and-orientation-changing love (still going strong!), has already made sense to other younger more apparently conventional couples. Even if not all were expressly written as epithalamia, the love poems here have all been specially selected to be said out loud and make wonderful wedding poems. I like to think of them affirming their own lyrical and lovely sounds in grand churches, wee village kirks, registry offices, beaches, livingrooms, bedrooms . . .

Maybe you're Scottish, or one of you is, by birth, or by distant descent and feel that should be celebrated on the day when you and your significant other marry your fortunes together. If so, maybe you'll choose the strange and salty strong, strang, sound of Scots. Try Willie Hershaw's 'Welsh Love Spuin'; or Sheena Blackhall's 'Haunfast'; or Maureen Sangster's 'The Pledge'; or J.K. Annand's 'Aa My Thochts'; or the heartbreakingly beautiful 'O Wert Thou in the Cauld Blast' by Robert Burns. No one could ever call 1 Corinthians 13 a wedding day cliché in W.L. Lorimer's lovely Scots translation. Imagine a Californian wedding-grove and a new spin of mysteriousness and gravitas lent to the extract from *The Prophet* by its 'owreset intil Scots' by David Purves.

If you're both girls you may like to add Carol Ann Duffy's 'White Writing' to your handfasting? Who in love doesn't wish, with R.L. Stevenson, to make the beloved 'brooches and toys for your delight'? Ian Crichton Smith's 'Love Poem' to his own 'Dear girl in your white muffs and your red coat' has an ending of devastating beauty and terror, and he has translated from the Gaelic Sorley MacLean's 'Traighean' ('Shores'): 'And were we by the shelves of Staffin/ where the huge joyless sea is coughing/ stones and boulders from its throat,/ I'd build a fortified wall/ against eternity's savage howl.'

What is loving each other but a fortified wall against eternity's savage howl?

LIZ LOCHHEAD
March 2004

Haunfast

Somethin auld: the years afore
Somethin new: the morn's door
Somethin borraed: kirk, or haa
Somethin blue: sky clear o sna
As bricht as ony wattergaw
A cloodless future spent as twa

SHEENA BLACKHALL

borraed	*borrowed*
kirk	*church*
haa	*hall*
sna	*snow*
wattergaw	*rainbow*

Four Greetings

mirth of the eyes be yours
candour of speech be yours
sureness of touch be yours
dance of the mind be yours

the mist of the glen
the weight of the hours
suspicion, worry, caution
lift away from you

in the hollow of your meeting
on the slope of your reclining
at the gate of your parting
grace, warmth, resourcefulness

no fear within you
no loss upon you
no malice near you
the stars above you

THOMAS A. CLARK

O, Wert Thou in the Cauld Blast

O, wert thou in the cauld blast
    On yonder lea, on yonder lea,
My plaidie to the angry airt,
    I'd shelter thee, I'd shelter thee.
Or did Misfortune's bitter storms
    Around thee blaw, around thee blaw,
Thy bield should be my bosom,
    To share it a', to share it a'.

Or were I in the wildest waste,
    Sae black and bare, sae black and bare,
The desert were a Paradise,
    If thou wert there, if thou wert there.
Or were I monarch o the globe,
    Wi thee to reign, wi thee to reign,
The brightest jewel in my crown
    Wad be my queen, wad be my queen.

ROBERT BURNS

airt   *direction of wind*
bield   *shelter*

The Annunciation

Now in this iron reign
I sing the liberty
Where each asks from each
What each most wants to give
And each awakes in each
What else would never be,
Summoning so the rare
Spirit to breathe and live.

Then let us empty out
Our hearts until we find
The last least trifling toy,
Since now all turns to gold,
And everything we have
Is wealth of heart and mind,
That squandered thus in turn
Grows with us manifold.

Giving, I'd give you next
Some more than mortal grace,
But that you deifying
Myself I might deify,
Forgetting love was born
Here in a time and place,
And robbing by such praise
This life we magnify.

Whether the soul at first,
This pilgrimage began,
Or the shy body leading
Conducted soul to soul
Who knows? This is the most
That soul and body can,
To make us each for each
And in our spirit whole.

EDWIN MUIR

Poetry of Persons

We love each other utterly
in sharing what we do not have;
we find each other finally
in losing what we cannot save.

We keep each other continually
in taking what we dare not hold;
we win each other daringly
when every treasure has been sold.

We fill each other with good things
when we hunger for the least
and receive the cup of blessing
uninvited to the feast.

We bring each other healing
in the strong herbs of silence;
we hear each other speaking
in the quiet voice of distance.

We come to know each other
accepting what we do not know;
we come to choose each other
whom we'd chosen long ago.

We see each other perfectly
in the beholding of the night;
we trust each other lastingly
in the unfolding of the light.

We complete each other constantly
but grow to a new whole;
we form a part of all that is,
and all that is forms us a soul.

We love each other utterly
in sharing what we do not have;
we gather again abundantly
after the casting in the grave.

TESSA RANSFORD

Bidie-in

Application

O let me be your bidie-in
And keep you close within
As dearest kith and kin
I promise I'd be tidy in
Whatever bed or bunk you're in
I'd never ever drink your gin
I'd be your multi-vitamin
I'd wear my sexy tiger-skin
And play my love-sick mandolin
It cannot be a mortal sin
To be in such a dizzy spin
I'd like to get inside your skin
I'd even be your concubine
I hope you know I'm genuine
O let me be your bidie-in.

bidie-in   *live-in partner*

Appointment

Of course, you may be my bidie-in,
You didn't need to apply within.
A braw new world's about to begin,
We'll gang thegether through thick and thin,
We'll walk unscathed through burr and whin.
If you're to be my porcupin
I'll just have to bear it and grin.
I'll be your sheik, your djinn,
I'll be yang to your yin.
You'll be my kitten, my mitten, my terrapin.
All night long we'll make love's sweet din
And never mind the wheelie-bin.
In our romantic cin-
ema there'll be no FIN.
And so I say again – you're in –
You've got the job of bidie-in!

DIANA HENDRY and HAMISH WHYTE

Tràighean

Nan robh sinn an Talasgar air an tràigh
far a bheil am beul mòr bàn
a' fosgladh eadar dà ghiall chruaidh,
Rubha nan Clach 's am Bioda Ruadh,
sheasainn-sa ri taobh na mara
ag ùrachadh gaoil nam anam
fhad 's a bhiodh an cuan a' lìonadh
camas Thalasgair gu sìorraidh:
sheasainn an siud air lom na tràghad
gu 'n cromadh Preiseal a cheann àigich.

Agus nan robh sinn cuideachd
air tràigh Chalgaraidh am Muile,
eadar Alba is Tiriodh,
eadar an saoghal 's a' bhiothbhuan,
dh'fhuirichinn an siud gu luan
a' tomhas gainmhich bruan air bhruain.
Agus an Uibhist air tràigh Hòmhstaidh
fa chomhair farsaingeachd na h-ònrachd,
dh'fheithinn-sa an siud gu sìorraidh,
braon air bhraon an cuan a' sìoladh.

Agus nan robh mi air tràigh Mhùideart
còmhla riut, a nodhachd ùidhe,
chuirinn suas an co-chur gaoil dhut
an cuan 's a' ghaineamh, bruan air bhraon dhiubh.
'S nan robh sinn air Mol Steinnseil Stamhain

Shores

If we were in Talisker on the shore
where the great white foaming mouth of water
opens between two jaws as hard as flint –
the Headland of Stones and the Red Point –
I'd stand forever by the waves
renewing love out of their crumpling graves
as long as the sea would be going over
the Bay of Talisker forever;
I would stand there by the filling tide
till Preshal bowed his stallion head.

And if the two of us were together
on the shores of Calgary in Mull
between Scotland and Tiree,
between this world and eternity,
I'd stand there till time was done
counting the sands grain by grain.
And also on Uist, on Hosta's shore,
in the face of solitude's fierce stare,
I'd remain standing, without sleep,
while sea were ebbing, drop by drop.

And if I were on Moidart's shore
with you, my novelty of desire,
I'd offer this synthesis of love,
grain and water, sand and wave.
And were we by the shelves of Staffin

24   's an fhàirge neo-aoibhneach a' tarraing
     nan ulbhag is gan tilgeil tharainn,
     thogainn-sa am balla daingeann
     ro shìorraidheachd choimhich 's i framhach.

SOMHAIRLE MACGILL-EAIN

where the huge joyless sea is coughing
stones and boulders from its throat,
I'd build a fortified wall
against eternity's savage howl.

SORLEY MACLEAN
translated by IAIN CRICHTON SMITH

Aa My Thochts
(*All mein Gedanken*. Bavarian folksong, c. 1460)

Aa the thochts that eir I hae, are thochts o ye.
My ane and only solace, be ye aye true to me!
Ye, ay, ye, soud hain me in your hert.
Gif I had my dearest wish
We twa wad never ever pairt.

My ane and only solace, think ye on this, my ain,
My life and gear will aye be yours alane to hain.
Yours, ay, yours, sall I forever be,
Ye are my smeddum and my joy,
Frae sorrow ye can make me free.

J. K. ANNAND

thochts	*thoughts*
soud hain	*should hold*
gif	*if*
gear	*possessions*
smeddum	*energy, spirit*

'I will make you brooches'

I will make you brooches and toys for your delight
Of bird-song at morning and star-shine at night.
I will make a palace fit for you and me
Of green days in forests and blue days at sea.

I will make my kitchen, and you shall keep your room,
Where white flows the river and bright blows the broom,
And you shall wash your linen and keep your body white
In rainfall at morning and dewfall at night.

And this shall be for music when no one else is near,
The fine song for singing, the rare song to hear!
That only I remember, that only you admire,
Of the broad road that stretches and the roadside fire.

ROBERT LOUIS STEVENSON

Seven Blessings

More to share than to possess
Words that refresh
The forgiving caress
The heart undressed.
Grace to cherish
Friendship to nourish
Love to flourish

DIANA HENDRY

The Confirmation

Yes, yours, my love, is the right human face.
I in my mind had waited for this long,
Seeing the false and searching for the true,
Then found you as a traveller finds a place
Of welcome suddenly amid the wrong
Valleys and rocks and twisting roads. But you,
What shall I call you? A fountain in a waste,
A well of water in a country dry,
Or anything that's honest and good, an eye
That makes the whole world bright. Your open heart,
Simple with giving, gives the primal deed,
The first good world, the blossom, the blowing seed,
The hearth, the steadfast land, the wandering sea,
Not beautiful or rare in every part,
But like yourself, as they were meant to be.

EDWIN MUIR

Ora nam Buadh

Ionnlaime do bhasa
Ann am frasa fiona,
Ann an liu nan lasa,
Ann an seachda siona,
Ann an subh craobh,
Ann am bainne meala,
Is cuirime na naoi buaidhean glana caon,
Ann do ghruaidhean caomha geala,

      Buaidh cruth,
      Buaidh guth,
      Buaidh rath,
      Buaidh math,
      Buaidh chnoc,
      Buaidh bhochd,
      Buaidh na rogha finne,
      Buaidh na fior eireachdais,
      Buaidh an deagh labhraidh.

Is dubhar thur ri teas,
Is seasgar thu ri fuachd,
Is sùilean thu dhan dall,
Is crann dhan deòraidh thruagh,
Is eilean thu air muir,
Is cuisil thu air tir,
Is fuaran thu am fàsach,
      Is slàinte dhan tì tha tinn.

Invocation of the Graces

I bathe thy palms
   in the elements seven,
With flowing water
   warmed by flame –
On the stone of the hearth
   'neath the arch of Heaven :
I fill thy shells, with a shower of wine,
   with raspberry juice and honeyed cream;
And I place the pure, choice graces nine
   in thy fair fond face :

        Grace of form,
        Grace of voice;
        Grace of fortune,
        Of goodly choice;
        Grace of skill,
        Of loving will;
        Grace of girlhood white,
        Of whole-souled beauty bright,
   And grace of winning words.

A shade art thou in the heat,
   A shelter art thou, in cold;
A staff to wandering feet,
   Eyes to the blind and old;
A castle art thou on land,

32

Is tu sonas gach ni èibhinn,
Is tu solus gath na grèine,
Is tu dorus flath na fèile,
Is tu corra reul an iùil,
Is tu ceum fèidh nan àrdaibh,
Is tu ceum steud nam blàraibh,
Is tu sèimh eal an t-snàmha,
     Is tu àilleagan gach rùn.

Cruth àlainn an Dòmhnaich
Ann do ghnuis ghlain,
An cruth is àilinde
Bha air talamh.

An tràth is feàrr san latha dhut,
An là as feàrr san t-seachdain dhut,
An t-seachdain is feàrr sa bhliadhna dhut,
A' bhliadhn' is feàrr an domhan Mhic Dhè dhut.

extract from *Carmina Gadelica*

On ocean thou'rt an isle;
In the wilderness, a well,
    Their health to all who ail.

O thou art the joy in every delight!
    Thou art the light of a first sunbeam;
Thou art the guiding star by night,
    And the glow through the gates of a welcoming
    chief:
Thou art the step of the deer on the height
    And the step of a mettlesome steed on the field :
Thou art the calm of the gliding swan :
    of longings thou'rt the loveliness.

The lovely likeness of the Lord
    is in thy pure face,
The loveliest form
    was e'er on earth.

The best hour of the day be thine,
The best day of the seven be thine,
The best seven of the year be thine,
And the best of the years of our Lord, be thine.

translated by ARTHUR GEDDES

NOTE: *This is an extract from the translation by Dr. Arthur Geddes of the Gaelic prayer 'Ora nam Buadh'; a poem for a girl on the eve of marriage, composed perhaps by her father.*

These Rings

These rings that we exchange
renew themselves as the unwearied surf
that garlands but never binds
the coastline of an island
from which love ever sails
towards the horizon's circle
always farther
beyond which we cannot reach
and all of these
are emblems of our taking of each other
no more constricted
than is the earth
by the enfolding of the sea.

GAEL TURNBULL

Mairi's Wedding

Step we gaily, on we go,
Heel for heel and toe for toe,
Arm in arm and row in row,
All for Mairi's wedding.

Over hillways up and down,
Myrtle green and bracken brown,
Past the shielings, thro' the town;
All for sake of Mairi.

chorus

Red her cheeks as rowans are,
Bright her eyes as any star,
Fairest o' them a' by far
Is our darling Mairi.

chorus

Plenty herring, plenty meal,
Plenty peat to fill her creel,
Plenty bonny bairns as weel;
That's the toast for Mairi.

chorus

SIR HUGH ROBERTON

| shielings | *farmsteads* |
| creel | *basket* |

With These Rings

You are fresh words
on the old stone of time.

Here, silence honours you,
here now, the earth turns,
the sun beats, the rain sings.

You are not adrift
among the wheeling constellations
but held by the hoop of love.

Ancient as the ring of standing stones,
prophetic as a snow-ring round the moon,
marriage is.

Wear your vows well when laughter
is the wine between you

or when night lies like a bolster
down the middle of your bed.

May the cold shoulder of the hill
always afford you shelter.
May the sun always seek you
however dark the place.

We who are wordless know
thorns have roses.

And when you go from this day
the burnished stars go with you.

When you go forward from this day,
the love that grew you
grows with you

and marriage is struck,
iron on stone, hand in hand.

JANET PAISLEY

Wi Thur Twa Rings

Yeese are chippit new
intae the auld stane o time.

Here, awthing faws quate fur yeese,
here noo, sunlicht skirls,
rain diddles, the yirth birls.

Yeese are no alane
amang the hurlin constellations
but cleikit tae thon gird cried love.

Aulder than ony circle o staunin stanes,
shair as a snaw-ring roon the mune,
mairrige is.

Weer yer vows weel when kecklin
is the ale atween yeese

or when nicht draps like a bolster
doon the middle o yer bed.

Let the cauld shooder o the ben
aywis coorie ye kindly.
Let the sun aywis hunt ye
hooever daurk yon place.

We wha haud oor wheesht ken
thorns hae roses.

And when ye gang fae this day
the skinklin staurs gang wi ye.

When ye gang furrit fae this day,
the love that grew ye
growes wi ye

and mairrige is wrocht,
iron oan stane, haund in haund.

JANET PAISLEY

Songline

Continents divide us,
many song-lines
crossed.
Slender melodies,
air-spun, high-wheeling,
begun on a Scottish island,
converse in intimate harmony,
binding family together.
A love-poem, migrating like a bird,
seeks the warmth of your smile.
It is blown on a wish-wind,
halfway round the world,
to sing at your wedding.

LIS LEE

An Autumn Wedding Song

The shepherd's woollens match his flock
and salmon swam that we should dine.
Time sticks this once within the clock
while distant slopes provide fine wine

and Gala Water flows to Tweed

Doves sound as morning rides the trees.
Red swags of rowan, ruddy apples
assert their ripe fertilities
as mellowed whisky eases thrapples

and supple Tweed runs to the sea

Sun and stripped field delight in meeting
and while each leaf is timed to drop
all shout their green to golden greeting.
Spring's gifts crowd autumn's table top.

At Berwick nations bridge and marry

When matching seems both strong and wise
its place is neither grand nor small.
Sufficient in wellwishing eyes
that there are ample sweets for all.

Bright ocean rolls to further seas

ANGUS CALDER

Catullus LXI

Pit by the time for bydin:
  By Venus you are blest.
  Hit's clear to ilka guest
Whit force steirs groom and bride in
A luve that's no for hidin.

Wha numbers the sands o Afrikie
  Or the glisterin stars their names,
Wad find mair trauchle gin that he
Ettled to tot up eidently
  Your mony-thoosand randy games.

Pley weill, mak luve; lat your flesh mell
That it perpetuates itsel:
  Sic bonny young anes as you are
  Honour your forefolk when you gar
Your growthie bodies rise and swell.

Lassies, sneck the yett:
  The jiggin's ower, we're awa hame,
But you, newly conjoinit,
  Big braw lad and sonsie dame:
You'll pairty on through life, I'll bet.

Transcreation: TOM HUBBARD
NOTE: *Inspired by Catullus (c.84-c.54 B.C.), whose original
epithalamium is one of the oldest wedding poems in the world.*

pit	*put*
bydin	*waiting, delaying*
hit's	*it's (this aspiration is common in south Fife)*
steirs	*stirs*
glisterin	*glittering*
trauchle	*trouble, grind (in the sense of hard work that has to be endured)*
gin	*if (hard g)*
ettled	*tried, attempted*
eidently	*diligently*
gar	*make, cause [... to]*
growthie	*fertile, abundant*
sneck	*lock, fasten*
yett	*gate, large door*
jiggin	*dancing*
braw	*impressive, good-looking*
sonsie	*buxom*

The Wedding Reel

True love which lovers promise has one aim:
if you are two, then you'll be two the same

As plants that grow around the tree in vines
where shoots climb elms to shelter from the wind

As king and queen are printed on a suit of cards
in every game they play with their whole Hearts

As ring and finger from today will go together
fitting two hands, handfast to one another

As silver buckles on a belt are clasped
so linked in love they'll live and hold at last

As two streams flow to join the greater river
the land between is fruitful, blessed for ever

As verse and tune match one harmonious ideal
you'll dance barefoot in the first wedding reel

The love which lovers promise to themselves is meant
to make two separate pasts become a single present.

VALERIE GILLIES

Epithalamium for Joe and Annie Thomson

For Marriage, love and love alone's the argument.
Sweet ceremony, then hand in hand we go
Taking to our changed, still dangerous days,
   our complement.
We think we know ourselves, but all we know
Is: love surprises us. It's like when sunlight flings
A sudden shaft that lights up glamorous the rain
Across a Glasgow street – or when Botanic Spring's
First crisp, dry breath turns February air champagne.

Delight's infectious – your quotidian friends
Put on, with gladrag finery today, your joy,
Renew in themselves the right true ends
They won't let old griefs, old lives destroy.
When at our lover's feet our opened selves we've laid
We find ourselves, and all the world, remade.

LIZ LOCHHEAD

Journey

Today you see far down a mountainside,
out over islands to your far horizon.
Your sight is sharp, your goal clear, and tides
of love lap round all your desiring.

Two sets of footprints you will make, but true
companions on this journey you'll become.
When you slip out of step, think of today;
relive again its close embrace of freedom.

May truest feelings stir you as the wind
disturbs the loch, or smirr on cotton grass.
May you find bliss in ordinariness
and joy forever in its present tense.

CHRISTINE DE LUCA

smirr   *fine rain*

A Winter Wedding

Last autumn's heather
and the snowdrops yet to be
even by their absence
join to celebrate
both what outlasts
and what anticipates
as we two shall
look neither back nor forward
but to each other
on this brief day
and longest night for festival.

GAEL TURNBULL

On Mairriage

Luve ither, but makna
  a thirldom o luve:
Lat it be lyker a rowin swaw
  atween the forelands o yeir sauls.
Fill ither's cup,
  but drinkna frae the ae cup.
Gie ither frae yeir breid,
  but dinna eat frae the same laif.
Sing and dance thegither an be blyth,
  but lat ilkane be alane,
even as the fiddle strings is sindert,
  tho thai dirl the same muisic.

Gie yeir herts,
  but no intil ither's keepin.
For anerlie the haund o Lyfe
  can haud yeir herts.
An staun aye thegither,
  yit no owre near:
For the pillars o the temple
  stauns aye apairt,
An the aik an the cypress
  growes ootby ither's shaidae.

from *The Prophet* by KAHLIL GIBRAN
owreset intil Scots bi DAVID PURVES

ither	*each other*
thirldom	*bondage*
lyker	*more like*
rowin	*rolling*
swaw	*wave*
yeir	*your*
laif	*loaf*
ilkane	*each one*
sindert	*apart*
dirl	*vibrate*
anerlie	*only*
haud	*hold*
staun	*stand*
owre	*too*
aik	*oak*
ootby	*outside*
shaidae	*shadow*

Love Poem

The ways will never part
for us, I tell you now.
I write this in November
among the autumn leaves
the masks of Halloween,
that red Remembrance day.

We have had too much frost
and high snow together.
It is time for us to say;
This ring which once was salt
breeds blossoms round the bone,
and a whole life's union.

The sea stormy above
is always calm beneath.
The anchor will still hold
though the yachts dance and froth
in tantrums near the shore,
their masts like matchsticks.

For though it's autumn now
the trees will soon put on
their green crowns once more
as we too shall do
however weasels hunt
in the thick undergrowth.

Dear girl in your white muffs
and your red coat, I swear
no gaunt wolf from my heart
shall ever eat you up
except through love alone,
through love's most devious ways

and we two, hand in hand,
shall walk through all the mirrors
unsplintered to the end,
till only the bones remain
to stand up in all weathers
under the haunting wind.

IAIN CRICHTON SMITH

The Pledge

If we cud fly – an I feel we cud -
We'd look doon here tae where we're stood
Like twa braw trees in a widd –
Oor fruit, the handsome berry!
For in the past whan winds wid blaw
An smoory wis the fell snaw
An the sullen rains widna gang awa,
I cudna hairst the berry.

Bit noo, Love loves you an me;
Life's green an dancin like a tree;
Naethin will wither what's tae be –
Oor love'll bring us plenty.
Though Time'll try wi dolefu grey
Tae mak a mockery o today,
We'll hae, o'er Time, the final say –
This pledge, oor Love's bricht berry!

MAUREEN SANGSTER

cud	*could*
widd	*wood*
smoory	*enveloping*
fell	*severe*
hairst	*harvest (verb)*

NOTE: *The couple can read alternate lines, and then one together; for example, lines 1 and 3 read by one speaker, line 2 by the other, and line 4 in unison.*

epithalamium

this is your new garden, a whole wide
world of it, so green and songbird fresh,
all yours to map and fill with luminous
constellations of fruit and berry blossoms

this is your new garden, tend it as if
all the young shoots that promise
a succulent harvest of root and ear
will be young and tender for all time

this is your garden, there will always be
much hoeing and raking, the clearing
of weeds and sowing of seeds will ask
patience, attention, forgiving laughter

this is the garden you want to live in, it's not
all sunshine – there's moonshine too, all earth
needs storms, but when dark clouds peel back,
see your garden bloom into a universe of stars

AONGHAS MACNEACAIL

Welsh Love Spuin

A dunnlin bell, for oor weddin tryst,
A carved hert, for aw the love we hae,
A handfu o keys, for the hame that we big,
Raxin vines, for the hairst o oor love,
A birlin wheel, for aw the work we dae thegither,
A cleek, for us ayebidin.
Strang linkit chains, though the cauld hand o Deith
    tries ti pairt us.

Nae langer alane, ti bide as ane,
Wi an unco lang spuin ti sup the gowd brose
That's cawed Love.

WILLIAM HERSHAW

spuin	*spoon*
dunnlin	*ringing*
big	*build*
raxin	*reaching out*
hairst	*harvest*
birlin	*turning*
cleek	*latch*
unco	*unusually*
gowd	*gold*

White Writing

No vows written to wed you,
I write them white,
my lips on yours,
light in the soft hours of our married years.

No prayers written to bless you,
I write them white,
your soul a flame,
bright in the window of your maiden name.

No laws written to guard you,
I write them white,
your hand in mine,
palm against palm, lifeline, heartline.

No rules written to guide you,
I write them white,
words on the wind,
traced with a stick where we walk on the sand.

No news written to tell you,
I write it white,
foam on a wave
as we lift up our skirts in the sea, wade,

see last gold sun behind clouds,
inked water in moonlight.
No poems written to praise you,
I write them white.

CAROL ANN DUFFY

1 Corinthians 13

Luve is pâtientfu; luve is couthie an kind;
luve is nane jailous; nane sprosie;
nane bowdent wi pride; nane mislaired;
nane hame-drauchtit; nane toustie.

Luve keeps nae nickstick o the wrangs it drees;
finnds nae pleisur i the ill wark o ithers;
is ey liftit up whan truith dings líes;
kens ey tae keep a caum souch;
is ey sweired tae misdout;
ey howps the best; ey bides the warst.

There is three things bides for ey:
faith, howp, luve.
But the grytest o the three is luve.

from *The New Testament in Scots*
by W. L. LORIMER

couthie	*sympathetic*
sprosie	*boastful*
bowdent	*swollen*
mislaired	*misguided*
hame-drauchtit	*selfish*
toustie	*irritable*
drees	*endures*
dings	*strikes down*
keep a caum souch	*keep quiet*
sweired tae misdout	*reluctant to disbelieve*

Gaelic Blessing

Beannachd Dhè a bhith agaibh,
'S guma math a dh'èireas dhuibh;
Beannachd Chriosda a bhith agaibh,
'S guma math a chuirear ruibh;
Beannachd Spioraid a bhith agaibh,
'S guma math a chuireas sibh seachad bhur saoghal,
Gach latha dh'èireas sibh a suas,
Gath oidhche laigheas sibh a slos.

God's blessing be yours,
and well may it befall you;
Christ's blessing be yours,
And well be you entreated;
Spirit's blessing be yours,
And well spend you your lives,
Each day that you rise up,
Each night that you lie down.

from *Carmina Gadelica*
translated by ALEXANDER CARMICHAEL

There will be no end

There will be no end to the joy, my love.
We will stand together as the stars
sweep the Cuillin, rounding into morning
the bright new morning of the tender heart.
And where we sing, the songs will be a fine one
and where we dance, our steps will never fail
to tap the spring of life, of love and laughter
timeless as stars, the wheeling, circling stars
that dance and sing, and sing and dance again:
and there will be no end
to the joy

ANNE MACLEOD

MARGOT ROBERT ADAMSON (1898-?) wrote poetry and novels, and translated early Scots and English poetry from the Bannatyne and other manuscripts into modern English in *A Treasury of Middle-English Verse* (Dent, 1930).

J.K. ANNAND (1908-1993) was born and brought up in Edinburgh. His bairn rhymes continue to delight Scots children, but he was also the author of poetry for adults, and an active promoter of the Scots language. His *Selected Poems 1925-1990* was published by Mercat Press in 1992.

SHEENA BLACKHALL (b.1947) is a poet, writer, and folk-singer from Aberdeen. She has published many books of short stories and poetry in Scots, including *Stagwyse* (Charles Murray Trust, 1995) and *The Singing Bird: Poems* (GKB Books, 2000), and from 1999 to 2003 was Creative Writing Fellow in Scots at the Elphinstone Institute, University of Aberdeen.

ROBERT BURNS (1759-1796) is known and loved as Scotland's national bard. He was born in Ayrshire, the son of a farmer, and achieved his first success with the publication of *Poems, Chiefly in the Scottish Dialect* in 1786. His sublime love poems are translated into many languages; he himself was at home writing in English or Scots, and in many different verse forms. Burns served Scotland well both as poet and as a dedicated collector of the country's ballads and song.

ANGUS CALDER (b.1942), historian, journalist, editor and critic, has held academic posts in Britain and as far afield as New Zealand and Zimbabwe. A prolific author of works on socio-political themes, he has also always written poetry, bringing out his first book, *Waking in Waikato* (diehard) in 1997, followed by *Colours of Grief* (Shoestring Press, 2002).

ALEXANDER CARMICHAEL (1832-1912) gathered together between 1855 and 1899, largely from the Western Isles, a magnificent collection of Gaelic lore which was published as *Carmina Gadelica* (in five volumes, 1900-1954). The *Carmina* is mostly in the form of verse, with prayers, blessings, and work songs, accompanied by extensive notes and Carmichael's translations into English.

THOMAS A. CLARK (b.1944) was born in Greenock, spent many years in England, and has now returned to Scotland, where 'the different landscapes of the Highlands and Islands have been the central preoccupation of his poetry'. His collections include *Tormentil and Bleached Bones* (Polygon, 1993), *Distance and Proximity* (pocketbooks, 2000), and many small publications from Moschatel Press, his artist's book press in Fife.

CHRISTINE DE LUCA (b.1947) was born and brought up in Shetland. Now living in Edinburgh, she writes in both Shetland dialect and English, and the Shetland Library has published three books of her poetry, the most recent being *Plain Song* (2002). Her poems have been translated into several languages, and published in both national and international magazines.

CAROL ANN DUFFY (b.1955) was born in Glasgow but grew up in England, and now lives in Manchester, where she lectures at Manchester Metropolitan University. She has won the Forward and Whitbread prizes for poetry, is an acclaimed playwright, and was awarded a CBE in 2002. Her many books of poetry include *The World's Wife* (Picador, 1999), *Feminine Gospels* (Picador, 2002), and several collections for children.

ARTHUR GEDDES (1895-1968) was a geographer who worked first in India and France, then in Scotland at Edinburgh University. He published his translations of Gaelic songs from the Highlands and Islands in *The Songs of Craig and Ben* (2 vols; Vol.II William MacLellan, 1961); he also translated some of the Bengali songs of Rabindranath Tagore.

VALERIE GILLIES (b.1948) was born in Canada and brought up in Edinburgh, where she now lives. She has studied in India, worked as a poet and scriptwriter for radio and television, and held various writing fellowships and residencies. She teaches creative writing in schools, colleges and hospitals. Her recent publications include *Men and Beasts* (with photographer Rebecca Marr, Luath, 2000) and *The Lightning Tree* (Polygon, 2002).

DIANA HENDRY (b.1941) grew up in England but now lives in Edinburgh. She has worked as a journalist, teacher of English, and tutor of creative writing, and was Writer in Residence at Dumfries & Galloway Royal Infirmary. Her most recent poetry collections are *Borderers* (Peterloo Poets, 2001) and *Twelve Lilts; Psalms and Responses* (Mariscat, 2003). Of her many books for children, her novel, *Harvey Angell*, won a Whitbread Award in 1991. She first met Hamish Whyte in the Scottish Poetry Library.

WILLIAM HERSHAW (b.1957) is a teacher of English and folk musician in Fife. He writes mainly in Scots, and has published several collections of poetry, including *The Cowdenbeath Man* (Scottish Cultural Press, 1997). In 2003 he was the winner of the Callum Macdonald Memorial Poetry Pamphlet Prize with *Winter Song* (Touch the Earth, 2002).

TOM HUBBARD (b.1950) is a librarian, poet, editor and translator, who has taught Scottish literature at universities in Europe and the USA. Librarian of the Scottish Poetry Library 1984-1992, he has been editor of the Bibliography of Scottish Literature in Translation, based at the National Library of Scotland. In 2003 he co-edited *Stevenson's Scotland* (Mercat Press); the latest of his own publications are *From Soda Fountain to Moonshine Mountain* (Akros, 2004), and *Scottish Faust* (Kettillonia, 2004).

LIS LEE, a former journalist, is a poet and playwright, now in the Scottish Borders after living on the Isle of Mull for several years. Her work has been published in Scottish literary magazines, and in her own collection *Genie and Metaphor* (2003). *'Songline'* was written for her daughter's wedding in Australia.

LIZ LOCHHEAD (b.1947) has firmly established her reputation as one of the country's leading poets, and as a popular performer of her own poetry. She studied and taught art in Glasgow before becoming a full-time writer, publishing her first collection of poems, *Memo for Spring*, in 1972. Also a playwright, her adaptation of Euripides' *Medea* (2000) won the Saltire Society's Scottish Book of the Year Award. *The Colour of Black & White: Poems 1984 – 2003* (Polygon, 2003) is Liz Lochhead's first collection of poetry for over a decade.

WILLIAM LAUGHTON LORIMER (1885-1967) had a distinguished career teaching Greek, culminating in holding the Chair of Greek at St Andrews University. The pinnacle of his life's study of Scots is his masterly translation of the New Testament from Greek into Scots, which was published in 1983, the editing having been completed by his son, R.L.C. Lorimer.

SORLEY MACLEAN / SOMHAIRLE MACGILL-EAIN (1911-1996) is undoubtedly the greatest Gaelic poet of the twentieth century. He was born on the island of Raasay, and Gaelic was his mother tongue. Having learnt English at school, he went on to study it at university, but was active in preserving the teaching of Gaelic in schools from the 1960s, and has been called the 'father of the Gaelic Renaissance'. His first book *Dàin do Eimhir agus Dàin Eile* was published by William MacLellan in 1943; a new edition by Christopher Whyte includes some previously uncollected poems from the series (ASLS, 2002). He received the Queen's Gold Medal for

Poetry in 1990, and the latest edition of his collected poems was published by Carcanet/Birlinn in 1999.

ANNE MACLEOD (b. 1951) studied medicine at Aberdeen University, and now works as a dermatologist in Inverness-shire. She is a novelist as well as a poet, her most recent collection of poetry being *Just the Caravaggio* (Poetry Salzberg, 1999)

AONGHAS MACNEACAIL (b.1942) was born on the Isle of Skye, and brought up in a Gaelic-speaking community. He has worked in radio and film, and often collaborated with musicians and artists. An active campaigner for the Gaelic language, he writes in both English and Gaelic; his collection of poems *Oideachadh Ceart / A Proper Schooling* (Polygon, 1996) won the Stakis Prize.

EDWIN MUIR (1887-1959) was born in Orkney, but moved to Glasgow with his family when he was fourteen. His poetic vision is strongly influenced by a longing for lost Edens and lost childhood, as well as his apocalyptic sense of war and its aftermath. An influential critic as well as poet, he published seven volumes of poetry, collected together in *The Complete Poems of Edwin Muir* (Faber, 1991).

JANET PAISLEY (b.1948) grew up in central Scotland where she still lives. Her publications include five collections of poetry, the most recent being *Ye Cannae Win*, (Chapman, 2000); two of short stories; plays for theatre and radio; TV drama, and film. Her work has been widely translated. She originally wrote 'With These Rings' for the wedding of one of her sons, and has since set it into Scots.

DAVID PURVES (b. 1924) was born in Selkirk, took his degree at Edinburgh University, and followed a career as an agricultural chemist. Dr Purves has long been an activist in the cause of the Scots language, editing the magazine *Lallans* 1987-1995. He is a prolific translator into Scots of ancient Chinese and other poetry, and has written plays in Scots, as well as his own poetry, which was published in *Hert's Bluid* (Chapman, 1995).

TESSA RANSFORD (b.1938) worked for two decades to set up and sustain the School of Poets and the Scottish Poetry Library (before retiring at the millennium), for which services she was awarded an OBE, and spent a decade editing *Lines Review*. She continues as freelance poetry adviser and practitioner; works to encourage the publication of poetry in pamphlet form; and is President of Scottish PEN. The most recent of her eleven books of poetry is *When it Works it Feels Like Play* (Ramsay Head, 1998), and a series of pamphlet selections from *Akros*.

SIR HUGH ROBERTON (1874-1952), the author of the popular song 'Mairi's Wedding', was a conductor and composer who founded Glasgow's Orpheus Choir.

The original Gaelic words were written by John Bannerman for the Mod of 1935; Roberton wrote his English version the following year, and set it to a traditional tune.

MAUREEN SANGSTER (b.1954) was born in Aberdeen and lives in Fife. Her poetry is published in *Out of the Urn* (Scottish Cultural Press, 1997) and *The Unseen Hospital* (Kettillonia, 2002), a collection that grew out of a residency at Dumfries Royal Infirmary and Crichton Royal.

IAIN CRICHTON SMITH / IAIN MAC A' GHOBHAINN (1928-1998) was born on the island of Lewis, and spent most of his life as a schoolteacher in Glasgow and Oban, receiving an OBE in 1980. From *The Long River* (Macdonald, 1955) to *A Country for Old Men* (Carcanet, 2000), he was a prolific writer in both English and Gaelic, of poetry and fiction; a sense of exile is at the heart of his work. His view of Scotland's culture, small communities and religion was never romantic, but he had a keen eye for small delights and a strong sense of wonder.

ROBERT LOUIS STEVENSON (1850-1894), author of the well-loved tales *Treasure Island* and *Kidnapped*, was also a poet. His best-known collection is *A Child's Garden of Verses*, but Stevenson also wrote much lyric poetry, and a range of lively verse in Scots. He was born in Edinburgh, but – for the sake of his health - travelled and lived abroad, and is buried in Samoa. The most recent full edition of his poetry is *The Collected Poetry of Robert Louis Stevenson*, edited by Roger C. Lewis (Edinburgh University Press, 2003).

GAEL TURNBULL (1928-2004) was a medical practitioner in Britain, America and Canada, and returned to live in Edinburgh, where he was born. His work ranged from prose poetry and collage poems to his inventive 'poem-objects', but all express a 'delight in language and in the possibilities of utterance'. His published poetry is collected in *A Gathering of Poems 1950-1980* (Anvil,1983), *For Whose Delight* (Mariscat, 1995), *Might a Shape of Words* (Mariscat, 2000), and many smaller publications.

HAMISH WHYTE (b.1947) is a poet, publisher, editor, and former librarian. He has edited several anthologies of West of Scotland poetry, notably *Mungo's Tongues: Glasgow Poems 1630-1990* (Mainstream, 1993). He contributes to current poetry publishing in Scotland with his Mariscat Press, and is an Honorary Research Fellow at the Department of Scottish Literature, University of Glasgow. He first met Diana Hendry at the Scottish Poetry Library.

ACKNOWLEDGEMENTS

Our thanks are due to the following authors, publishers, and estates who have generously given permission to reproduce works:

J.K. Annand, 'Aa my Thochts' from *Selected Poems 1925-1990* (Mercat Press, 1992), reprinted by permission of Scottish Language Dictionaries;   Sheena Blackhall, 'Haunfast' copyright © 2004, printed by permission of the author; Angus Calder, 'An Autumn Wedding Song' copyright © 2004, printed by permission of the author; Thomas A. Clark, 'Four Greetings' (Moschatel Press, 1998), reprinted by permission of the author; Christine De Luca, 'Journey' copyright © 2004, printed by permission of the author; Carol Ann Duffy, 'White Writing' from *Feminine Gospels* (Picador, 2002), reprinted by permission of Macmillan Publishers Ltd.; Arthur Geddes, 'Invocation of the Graces' from *The Songs of Craig and Ben*, Vol.II (William MacLellan, 1961), reprinted by permission of Claire Geddes; Valerie Gillies, 'The Wedding Reel' copyright © 2004, printed by permission of the author; Diana Hendry, 'Seven Blessings' copyright © 2004, printed by permission of the author; Diana Hendry and Hamish Whyte, 'Bidie-In' (Uneven Press, 2002), reprinted by permission of Hamish Whyte; William Hershaw, 'Welsh Love Spuin' from *The Cowdenbeath Man* (Scottish Cultural Press, 1997), reprinted by permission of the author; Tom Hubbard, 'Catullus LXI' copyright © 2004, printed by permission of the author; Lis Lee, 'Songline' from *Genie and Metaphor* (2003), reprinted by permission of the author; Liz Lochhead, 'Epithalamion' from *The Colour of Black & White* (Polygon, 2003), reprinted by permission of Birlinn Ltd.; W.L. Lorimer, '1 Corinthians 13' from *New Testament in Scots* (Southside, 1983), reprinted by permission of Mrs. Priscilla Lorimer and the Trustees of the W.L. Lorimer Foundation; Sorley MacLean, 'Tràighean' from *O Choille gu Bearradh/From Wood to Ridge* (Carcanet/Birlinn, 1999) reprinted by permission of Carcanet Press Ltd.; Anne MacLeod, 'There Will be No End' from *Standing by Thistles* (Scottish Cultural Press, 1997), reprinted by permission of the author; Aonghas MacNeacail, 'epithalamium' copyright © 2004, printed by permission of the author; Janet Paisley, 'With These Rings'/'Wi Thur Twa Rings' copyright © 2004, printed by permission of the author; David Purves, 'On Mairriage' (*Lallans*, No.41, 1993) reprinted by permission of the author;   Tessa Ransford, 'Poetry of Persons' from *Light of the Mind* (Ramsay Head Press, 1980) reprinted by permission of the author and Ramsay Head Press; Hugh S. Roberton, 'Mairi's Wedding' (Hugh S. Roberton, © 1950), reprinted by permission of Roberton Publications; Maureen Sangster, 'The Pledge' copyright © 2004, printed by permission of the author; Iain Crichton Smith,'Love Poem' from *Orpheus and other Poems* (Akros, 1974), and 'XLII' (Shores') from *Eimhir* (Acair, 1999), reprinted by permission of Carcanet Press; Gael Turnbull, 'A Winter Wedding' and 'These Rings' from *From the Language of the Heart* (Gnomon Press, 1985), reprinted by permission of the author.